The Bathroom Fascinating Facts Book

by

Jack Kreismer

RED-LETTER PRESS, INC.
Saddle River, New Jersey

THE BATHROOM FASCINATING FACTS BOOK

ISBN: 9781603871631

Printed in the United States of America

Red-Letter Press, Inc.
P.O. Box 393
Saddle River, NJ 07458

www.Red-LetterPress.com

ACKNOWLEDGMENTS

EDITORIAL:
Jeff Kreismer

•

BOOK DESIGN & TYPOGRAPHY:
Jeff Kreismer

•

COVER ART:
Jeff Godby

•

RESEARCH & DEVELOPMENT:
Kobus Reyneke
Mike Ryan
Jim Tomlinson

The Bathroom Fascinating Facts Book

More than 10% of Americans claim to have seen UFOs, including one former president, Jimmy Carter.

❖

Frederick's of Hollywood introduced thong underwear to America in 1981.

❖

The average American walks between five and seven thousand steps per day.

❖

John Jay, the first Chief Justice of the Supreme Court, bought slaves just so he could free them.

❖

Like humans, dogs can be right-handed or lefthanded (or should that be south "paw"?).

❖

Donald Trump and Ronald Reagan are the only divorced presidents.

❖

Ann Royall became the first woman journalist to interview a president. While John Q. Adams was skinny-dipping one day, she stole his clothes and wouldn't give them back until he talked to her.

Thoughts of the Throne

Because it was built before desegregation, the Pentagon has twice the number of toilets needed for a building of its size.

Karate was not introduced to Japan until 1916. Until then, it had been practiced solely by Okinawans, who developed it centuries before as a weaponless defense.

❖

Ron Wayne sold his 10% stake in Apple computers for $500 in 1976.

❖

Caterpillars are a delicacy in Peru.

❖

Gamblers have the highest suicide-attempt rate.

❖

Two-thirds of the world's lawyers are in the good old US of A, as in attorneys.

❖

The "E" in Robert E. Lee stands for Edward.

❖

Falcons have "eagle eyes." They can see a ladybug on the ground from atop an 18-story building.

❖

The best-selling prepared dessert in the world is Jell-O.

Quick Quiz

According to *Guinness*, who is the world's most frequent clapper?

Vanna White, of TV's *Wheel of Fortune*, who claps her hands an average of 720 times per episode

Carrots have been white, black, purple, green and red. It wasn't until the 17th century that Denmark growers crossbred red and yellow carrots to create what is now the universal orange color.

❖

Elephants weigh up to 14,000 pounds.

❖

George Washington laid the cornerstone of the U.S. Capitol building.

❖

The International Lint Museum is in Rutland, Vermont.

❖

Yes, lima beans do come from Lima. They were brought here from Peru by U.S. Navy Captain John Harris in 1824.

❖

Garry Turner clipped 160 ordinary clothespins on his face for a world record on January 9, 2009.

❖

The smallest unit of length measurement in the world is the atto-meter, equivalent to a mere quintillionth of a centimeter.

THOUGHTS OF THE THRONE

The nickname "john" for a toilet is in honor of Englishman John Harrington, who devised the first flush mechanism near the end of the 16th century.

Only one out of three people who buy jogging shoes use them for that purpose.

❖

Andrew Jackson was the first Democratic Party presidential candidate in 1828. He won.

❖

Neophobia is the fear of anything new.

❖

3.2% of Americans are vegetarians.

❖

India has the largest vegetarian population in the world.

❖

The word "vegetarian" originated in 1847. Before that, a non-meat-eater was known as a pythagorean.

❖

There are no photographs that show Abraham Lincoln smiling.

❖

There is a club in the United States whose only membership requirement is that your name is Jim Smith.

Quick Quiz

In 2019, a Canadian team won an NBA championship for the first time. Name it.

Toronto Raptors

A bat's knees bend backwards.

❖

A typical dinner for a whale is 5,000 fish.

❖

Jousting is the official state sport of Maryland.

❖

Alaska's state flower is the forget-me-not.

❖

Greenland's official language is Danish.

❖

A Babe Ruth jersey was sold for a record $5.6 million in 2019.

❖

U.S. Patent Office records show that Thomas Jefferson invented the first hideaway bed.

❖

The A&M in Texas A&M stands for Agricultural and Mechanical.

❖

Bubble wrap was originally to be used as 3D wallpaper.

Thoughts of the Throne

Joseph Gayetty invented toilet paper in 1857 and we have British inventor Walter Alcock to thank for his 1879 ideas to perforate the paper and put it on a roll.

The BBC reports that someone with nothing better to do did a study which concluded that the average time high heels are kept on for is one hour, six minutes and 48 seconds.

❖

Street numbers in Japan are not assigned by the position of the house on the street, but by when the house was built. The older the house, the lower the street number, regardless of street location.

❖

On October 31, 1997, Violet Palmer became the first female NBA referee.

❖

Sarah Thomas became the first female NFL referee in 2015 and, in 2019, she became the first woman to be an official at a postseason game.

❖

Young spiders can regenerate missing legs and parts of legs.

❖

In Japan, only 4% of the population is left-handed.

❖

Cabbage is 91% water.

Quick Quiz

What electronics store was originally called Sound of Music?

Best Buy

The first woman to appear on the front of a Wheaties box was gymnast Mary Lou Retton, in 1984.

❖

The King of Hearts is the only king without a mustache in a deck of cards.

❖

In 1587, Virginia Dare became the first person born in America to English parents.

❖

While on his honeymoon in 1879, Robert Louis Stevenson wrote *Travels with a Donkey*. Naturally, his wife was flattered.

❖

The median length of a marriage in the U.S. is now just seven years.

❖

The male fox mates for life. If the female dies, he will remain single for the rest of his life. However, if the male dies, the female will find another mate.

❖

548 peanuts are needed to make a 12-ounce jar of peanut butter.

Thoughts of the Throne

Leave it to Beaver was the first TV program to show a bathroom and a toilet. However, only the tank of the toilet was seen on the episode.

Charles Roser invented the Fig Newton.

❖

The male to female ratio of lefties is 2-1.

❖

10% of people are left-handed, 19% left-footed in America.

❖

3% of Americans hang family pictures in their bathrooms.

❖

A mole can dig a 300-foot long tunnel in one night.

❖

A hummingbird lays only two eggs during its lifetime.

❖

Elephants, when they've had one too many, can be terribly rowdy drunks.

❖

Voltaire drank 70 cups of coffee a day.

❖

A pottle is 2 quarts.

Quick Quiz

Who is Nadya Suleman and how many kids does she have?

She's known as "Octomom" after she gave birth to octuplets in 2009. She now has a total of 14 children.

Alan Shepard was the first astronaut to play golf on the moon.

❖

Ants do not sleep.

❖

Sportswriter Caswell Adams coined the name "Ivy League."

❖

If you hear a person saying words like "grundy," "blot" and "vetch," they are not having a seizure, but talking about the sport of frisbee.

❖

Hummingbirds can't walk.

❖

A housefly beats its wings an average of 20,000 times a minute.

❖

A grasshopper can jump about two feet.

❖

Tweety Pie was originally a pink canary, but censors complained that he looked naked, so his color was changed to yellow.

Thoughts of the Throne

According to a 2013 Michigan State University study, only 5% of people wash their hands enough to kill infection and illness-causing germs after using the bathroom.

One out of every ten paper clips is bought by the U.S. government.

❖

Women shoplift more often than men by a ratio of 4 to 1.

❖

The first beer brewed in the New World was brewed at Sir Walter Raleigh's Roanoke Colony in 1587. The beer kept its head longer than Sir Walter did!

❖

One-fourth of all the turkey eaten in the U.S. is gobbled down on Thanksgiving Day.

❖

Jackie Kennedy was the first First Lady to be born in the 20th century.

❖

Mark Twain called cauliflower "cabbage with a college education."

❖

A tomato is 95% water.

❖

97% of the earth's water is seawater.

Quick Quiz

Joey Chestnut wolfed down a record of how many hot dogs on July 4, 2018?
a) 34 b) 54 c) 74

Lee Harvey Oswald's weapon is stored in a rifle case on a shelf in Room 5W of the Judicial and Fiscal and Social Branch of the U.S. National Archives.

❖

From the police blotter: Ex-prez Franklin Pierce was once arrested for accidentally running down Mrs. Nathan Lewis while on horseback.

❖

A man in Jerusalem was arrested for speeding while using his elbows to steer the car as he spoke into cell phones he was using with both hands.

❖

Martha Giles of Newark, New Jersey, was granted a divorce on the grounds that her husband attacked her with a live eel.

❖

The Chicago Post Office at 433 W. Van Buren is the only drive through postal facility in the world.

❖

Strength is the only 8-letter word in the English language with only one vowel.

❖

Crows can live 80 years.

Thoughts of the Throne

In the mid-1800s, someone secured a patent for a toilet seat with rollers on top to prevent friends from standing on it. Why anyone would want to was not explained.

Most people are unable to speak more than 200 words per minute.

❖

The first air mail pilot ever took off and flew in the wrong direction, thus setting the standard for postal service to this very day.

❖

The home address of Charles Schulz was 1 Snoopy Place in Santa Rosa, California.

❖

Hershey, Pennsylvania, used to be known as Derry Church. Wonder if Derry Church Bars would ever have caught on?

❖

1.1% of Americans claim poultry as pets.

❖

The federal government once spent $50,000 to determine that the average length of a stewardess' nose is 2.6 inches.

❖

The number one bottled beverage in the U.S. is water. The average American drinks more than 42 gallons per year.

Quick Quiz

Who was Hillary Clinton's running mate when she won the popular vote in the presidential election but lost the electoral college vote to Donald Trump?

Tim Kaine

The U.S. Patent Office issued patent #1,180,753 for a device for catching female fish.

❖

At a rate of one drop a minute, a leaking faucet can waste 900 gallons of water a year.

❖

Every two weeks a lemon shark grows a new set of teeth. That's more than 24,000 new teeth each year.

❖

Atlanta, Georgia, was once known as Terminus.

❖

The butterfly is a cannibal.

❖

Smile and your Levator Labii Superioris Alaeque Nasi smiles with you. It is one of the primary muscles used for smiling.

❖

Aspirin was invented in Germany in 1853 but not marketed until 1899. Take two and call me in 46 years!

❖

Twenty six popes have been murdered.

Thoughts of the Throne

Legendary actress Joan Crawford changed toilet seats every time she changed husbands. That would be four times.

lifters are caught in December than any other month.

❖

Flies can get athlete's foot.

❖

Lake Mead is the largest man-made body of water in the western hemisphere.

❖

The most popular cookie is chocolate chip.

❖

A nun, Sister Mary Carolyn, was elected Mayor of Dubuque, Iowa, in 1980.

❖

Philadelphia originated the system of even-numbered residences on one side of the street and odd numbered homes on the other side.

❖

Al Jolson, in *The Jazz Singer*, spoke the first words on film- "Wait a minute! Wait a minute! You ain't heard nothing yet!"

❖

Monkeys never get fleas.

QUICK QUIZ

If you were to list all the countries in the world, which would come first and which would come last alphabetically?

Afghanistan and Zimbabwe

More people are injured on merry-go-rounds than roller coasters.

❖

The tropical catfish, synodontis, swims upside down while eating.

❖

Fish do not have a keen sense of hearing but they do have a keen sense of smell. Of course, much of what they smell is not that keen.

❖

There is no specific fish called a sardine. Usually you find herring or pilchard in the cans.

❖

You can put a good spin on a hardboiled egg, but not on an uncooked one.

❖

According to the International Dairy Foods Association, vanilla is the most popular flavor, second is chocolate and third is cookies 'n' cream.

❖

Seeing Eye dogs can poop on command. It's part of their training so that their blind owners know when to pick up what they've left behind.

Thoughts of the Throne

The first soap that floated on water was on the market in 1878. Manufactured by Proctor and Gamble, it was dubbed "White Soap" but a year later was given a new name- "Ivory Soap."

The "O" which Irish names begin with, such as O'Brien, simply means "son of." Therefore, O'Brien means son of Brien, the latter often being the name of the ancestor who started the family.

❖

Brontology is the study of thunder.

❖

Bugs Bunny was first called Happy Rabbit.

❖

Life Savers candy was invented the same year the Titanic sank- 1912.

❖

The sun and moon appear to be the same size in the sky because of an amazing coincidence- the moon is 400 times smaller but 400 times closer.

❖

Horses can look back with one eye and forward with the other. Because this can make them skittish, that's why they sometimes wear blinders.

❖

Horse racing legend Man O' War had a bad mare day when he suffered his only defeat- to a horse named Upset.

Quick Quiz

Triskaidekaphobics dread it when the first of the month falls on a Sunday. Why?

When the first of the month falls on a Sunday, there will always be a Friday the 13th- and triskaidekaphobia is a fear of that day.

Derby horse races are named after Edward Stanley, the 12th Earl of Derby, who created the special series of races for three-year-old horses.

❖

There are over nine million horses in the U.S. today.

❖

Alan Alda's real name is Alphonso Joseph D'Abruzzo.

❖

Rihanna's real name is Robyn Fenty.

❖

Pocahontas was a family nickname; her real name was Matoaka.

❖

There are no penguins at the North Pole. All varieties of penguins are found below the equator, mainly in Antarctica.

❖

The name of the first presidential aircraft, in 1944, was Sacred Cow.

❖

Caesar and Napoleon were both epileptics.

Thoughts of the Throne

President John F. Kennedy was in the bathtub when he put the finishing touches on his inaugural address.

An ex-president of the U.S. receives $207,800 annually in pension.

❖

Napoleon's hemorrhoids were a factor in his defeat at Waterloo. They kept him from being able to survey the battlefield on horseback.

❖

Peter the Great personally cut the beards of all his noblemen.

❖

Elephants can swim very well. They just have trouble keeping their trunks up.

❖

Wild sheep don't bear wool.

❖

The 1974 Bethel High School, Brandt, Ohio, football team just might be the worst ever. They were shut out in all 10 games: 40-0, 53-0, 92-0, 89-0, 50-0, 56-0, 36-0, 33-0, 46-0 and 49-0. The coach's name: Dennis Reck.

❖

The first edition of *The New York Times* appeared on September 18, 1851, and sold for a penny a pop.

Quick Quiz

What is a group of kittens called? (Hint: Think e-reader.)

A kindle

According to Nielsen, American adults are now spending almost six hours a day in front of a screen.

❖

62 out of 100 Americans say that the worst day of the week is- you guessed it- Monday.

❖

The second man to walk on the lunar surface was Buzz Aldrin. His mother's maiden name is Moon.

❖

The first president born in a hospital was Jimmy Carter.

❖

For some unknown reason, a duck's quack doesn't echo.

❖

According to a Gallup poll, the most hated food in America is liver.

❖

75% of optometrists wear eyeglasses.

❖

Most trips taken in the U.S. by car are less than five miles.

Thoughts of the Throne

A Scott Paper Company survey concluded that more than two-thirds of people with master's degrees and doctorates read in the bathroom.

Because his son-in-law was late with the carriage, Thomas Jefferson had to walk to his own inauguration.

❖

President Ulysses S. Grant was once arrested for exceeding the speed limit when driving a team of wild horses through the streets of Washington.

❖

Stainless steel can be rolled into strips thinner than human hair.

❖

Tiny hairs on the feet of flies act like taste buds as they stroll over your food.

❖

Marietta, Ohio, is named for Marie Antoinette.

❖

Every single pet hamster is a descendant from one female wild golden hamster found with a litter of 12 young in Syria in 1930.

❖

In 1976, 20 invited guests witnessed an official marriage ceremony between a Los Angeles secretary and a 50-pound rock.

Quick Quiz

Who was married to Auntie Em in *The Wizard of Oz*?

Uncle Henry

During a game of jai alai, the speed of the ball can reach 160 miles per hour.

❖

An elephant grows six sets of teeth during a lifetime.

❖

The Ouija board's name comes from combining the French and German words for "yes".

❖

The average American generates three pounds of garbage a day.

❖

Smokey Bear is the only one in America with his own zip code- 20252.

❖

Not to rain on your parade, but there are over one quadrillion ants living on the planet.

❖

Ants will not cross a white chalk line.

❖

When NBC plays three musical notes with its logo on TV, those notes are "G-E-C" for the General Electric Company, which owns the network.

Thoughts of the Throne

Actress Susan Sarandon proudly displays her Oscars and other awards in the bathroom. And Jodie Foster put her Oscar (Best Actress for her performance in *Silence of the Lambs*) in her bathroom next to the tub.

The reaction time of a cockroach is 54/1000 of a second, so you best not get into a gunfight with one.

❖

One out of four Americans is superstitious.

❖

According to a Gallup poll, 27% of Americans knock on wood.

❖

Playing the piano can use up more calories than doing light exercise.

❖

Last names in China are always one syllable.

❖

Pepto Bismol, when introduced in 1901, was called Mixture Cholera Infantum.

❖

A grasshopper's blood is white.

❖

Eleanor Roosevelt's maiden name was Roosevelt.

❖

West Point originated class rings.

Quick Quiz

If you spelled out the names of all 50 states, what's the only letter you wouldn't need?

Q

For 186 days a year, the sun is not seen at the North Pole.

❖

Onions can be stored for longer periods of time than any other vegetable.

❖

If you had a line of dimes 113.6 miles long, you'd be a millionaire!

❖

America's first billionaire was John D. Rockefeller, in 1911.

❖

New York City has the most billionaires in the world, Hong Kong is second among cities, and San Francisco is third.

❖

Eisenhower was known as an inveterate cat hater and ordered any cat found on his property shot on sight.

❖

Actor Robert Redford, singer Pat Boone and baseball legend Casey Stengel all have the same first name-Charles.

Thoughts of the Throne

President William Howard Taft was the heaviest chief executive, tipping the scales at 325 pounds. After repeatedly getting stuck in the White House bathtub, he had one installed big enough to accommodate four average-sized men.

Stogies get their name from the drivers of Conestoga wagons who often chomped on stubby cigars.

❖

Jacksonville, Florida, has the largest total area of any U.S. city, covering 874 square miles.

❖

The U.S. would fit into the continent of Africa three times.

❖

Boston was the first city in the U.S. with a subway.

❖

Garth, as in the singer Brooks, is his middle name. His first name is Troyal.

❖

Actress Jodie Foster's real first name is Alicia.

❖

At birth, a hippopotamus weighs about 100 pounds.

❖

Not long ago, a Bulgarian woman was allowed only one bath in her lifetime- and that was on the day before her wedding.

Quick Quiz

In Internet slang, what does ROTFL stand for?

Rolling On The Floor Laughing

Buckingham Palace is the former site of a brothel.

❖

Former baseball player Carlos May is the only big leaguer to have worn his birthday on his back. His number was 17 and his last name, which appeared above the number, read the same as the month in which he was born.

❖

According to Hallmark, the month with the most birthdays is August.

❖

The month with the fewest birthdays is- no surprise- February.

❖

J. Edgar Hoover would not allow anyone to walk on his shadow.

❖

Wall Street's name stems from colonial times when a wall was built around Lower Manhattan to protect cattle from Indian raids.

❖

Albert Einstein was four years old before he could talk.

Thoughts of the Throne

Green Bay, Wisconsin, claims to be the Toilet Paper Capital of the World.

Cows don't like spinach.

❖

The average American adult male is 5 feet 9 inches tall. The average woman is 5 feet 4 inches tall.

❖

The 1990 graduating class of the U.S. Navy's top school received diplomas stating they'd graduated from the Navel Academy.

❖

If you're cynophobic, you have a fear of dogs.

❖

Pepsi-Cola was originally called "Brad's Drink."

❖

A baby cockroach is called a "nymph."

❖

The average age at which a baby begins to deliberately smile is eight weeks.

❖

Donald Duck's nieces are April, May and June.

❖

The sleeve around a coffee cup is called a "zarf".

Quick Quiz

Which two U.S. presidents have double letters in both their first and last names?

Millard Fillmore and William Harrison

You are twice as likely to get a heart attack in winter than summer.

❖

Potato chips were invented in 1853 in Saratoga, New York, by George Crum.

❖

There's a 1 in 4 chance that an American will eat at a fast-food restaurant on any given day.

❖

According to Fast Food Nation, the average American will eat three hamburgers each week.

❖

When National League umpire Tom Gorman died in 1986, he was buried in his blue umpire's suit, and with a ball and strike indicator in his hand. The count on it was 3-2.

❖

In 1923, jockey Frank Hayes won a race at Belmont Park in New York despite being dead. He had a heart attack during the race, but his body stayed in the saddle until his horse crossed the line.

❖

A group of owls is called a parliament.

Thoughts of the Throne

A seat with no place to go: Until 1992, female U.S. Senators had no restroom. They were forced to use the tourists' ladies room of the building on Capitol Hill.

The maximum number of letters on one line of a *Wheel of Fortune* game board is 13.

❖

There are 35 species of coconuts.

❖

The soybean is the most versatile vegetable on earth, with over 400 different products made with it.

❖

In 1990, the California legislature overturned a ruling that allowed dogs' teeth to be cleaned only by veterinarians.

❖

The northernmost point in the continental U.S. is in Minnesota.

❖

Snakes don't blink.

❖

Tom Hanks has a collection of 250 typewriters.

❖

Charlotte Beysser Bartholdi was the model for the Statue of Liberty, which was sculpted by her son, Fredric Auguste Bartholdi.

QUICK QUIZ

What's the minimum age to be a United States Senator?

30

In an average lifetime, a person will grow over six feet of nose hair.

❖

Then and now: The average American used between 5 and 10 gallons of water in 1904. Today's American uses 80-100 gallons of water per day.

❖

John Adams, George Washington and Thomas Jefferson were avid marble collectors and players.

❖

In Ireland, if you donate a pint of blood, tradition has it that they give you a pint of Guinness to replace the iron.

❖

The Packard was the first car to cross the continent. It took 52 days in 1903.

❖

Honeybees are deaf.

❖

In 1931 Cleveland Indians catcher Joe Sprinz caught a baseball dropped 800 feet from a balloon. The impact created such a jolt through his body that he broke his jaw.

Thoughts of the Throne

The Beatles' George Harrison had a toilet seat which played *Lucy in the Sky with Diamonds.*

Timekeepers estimate that the action in a 60-minute football game actually amounts to 14 minutes.

❖

In the U.S. a baby is born every 8.5 seconds.

❖

According to the FDA, two out of five women dye their hair.

❖

You have a 1 in 600,000 chance of being struck by lightning sometime during your life.

❖

Irving Berlin was the only person in the history of the Academy of Motion Picture Arts and Sciences ever to present the Oscar to himself.

❖

If the wire of a Slinky was laid out flat, it would measure 67 feet.

❖

A shrimp's heart rules its head- probably because that's exactly where it is!

❖

Dr. Martin Luther King, Jr.'s first name was Michael.

Quick Quiz

True or False? The lower level of the George Washington Bridge is nicknamed Martha, after GW's wife.

True

The letters LED, as in digital, stand for "light-emitting diode."

❖

Baseball great Jackie Robinson's brother Mack finished second to Jesse Owens in the 200-meter race in the 1936 Olympics.

❖

The most popular crossword puzzle subject is the Bible.

❖

Soap Operas were so named because most of the sponsors were soap companies.

❖

Babe Ruth's real first name was George. So is Bob Newhart's. And so are the five sons of former heavyweight boxing champion George Foreman!

❖

Home plate in baseball was square until 1900, when it was made five-sided to help umpires in calling balls and strikes.

❖

Early American colonists made gray paint for their homes by boiling blueberries in milk.

Thoughts of the Throne

When Johnny Carson hosted *The Tonight Show*, he once joked about a scarcity of toilet paper during his monologue. It created a nationwide run on the product, causing a real shortage.

Wonder Bread introduced sliced bread in 1930.

❖

Just how fast is a snail's pace? About 25 feet per hour for most species.

❖

A soap bubble's wall is but a few millionths of an inch thick.

❖

Electric fans actually increase the temperature of the air.

❖

One pound of nickel can be stretched into a fine wire 80 miles long.

❖

Tiny earthworms have five hearts.

❖

There are 170,000,000,000,000,000,000,000,000 ways to play the ten opening moves in a chess game.

❖

Check out your computer keyboard and you'll notice there are three sets of letters in alphabetical order: f-g-h, j-k-l, and o-p.

Quick Quiz

How many dots, or pips as they are called, are there on a pair of dice?

42

The hippopotamus has skin two inches thick in some places.

❖

A football is made of cowhide, not pigskin.

❖

Michigan has the longest shoreline in the continental U.S.

❖

There are five counties in Texas that are larger than the state of Rhode Island.

❖

The highest sand dunes in the world are in the Sahara. They build up to a height of 1,410 feet.

❖

The geographic center of the U.S. is located near Castle Rock, South Dakota.

❖

Coca-Cola was banned from India in 1977 for refusing to disclose its secret formula.

❖

Men are eight times more likely to be colorblind than women.

Thoughts of the Throne

Agatha Christie said she came up with many of her book plots while sitting in her bathtub eating apples.

Heart attacks claim the fewest men on Fridays.

❖

Long before he got into big trouble for tax evasion, Pete Rose got into a little trouble for parking illegally outside Cincinnati's Riverfront Stadium. The street name on the ticket? Pete Rose Way.

❖

Mary Westmacott was the pen name of Agatha Christie when she was writing romantic novels.

❖

In the "gimme some space" department:
a "hairsbreadth away" is 1/48 of an inch.

❖

Teflon was called "fluon" when it was first discovered in 1938.

❖

Mickey Mouse has four fingers on each hand.

❖

Olive Oyl's measurements are 19-19-19.

❖

Of Pluto the former planet and Pluto the canine, the Disney dog was named first.

Quick Quiz

What's the name of the Pepperidge Farm Goldfish cracker mascot?

Finn

Rats can swim half a mile and tread water for three days.

If you suffer from polydactylism, you have more than your fair share of fingers or toes.

The most popular name for a pope is John. There have been 23 Pope Johns (25 if you count the two John Pauls).

Melt an ice cube in your mouth and you'll burn off 2.3 calories.

When he signed the statehood bills for North and South Dakota on the same day, President Benjamin Harrison wouldn't tell which one he signed first, so no one knows which is the 39th or 40th state.

Americans say their favorite color is blue, but the most popular car and house color is white.

According to Hoyle, poker is the national card game of the U.S.

Thoughts of the Throne

A newspaper in St. John, New Brunswick, Canada, once reported that a man was sentenced to 30 days in jail for stealing three boxes of Ex-Lax. His name: Frederick Andrew Outhouse.

Bela Lugosi is buried in his black Dracula cape.

❖

One of Thomas Jefferson's many inventions was the swivel chair.

❖

Andrew Jackson's pet parrot was in attendance at the former president's burial service but had to be removed for screeching profanities.

❖

George Washington, the "Father of Our Country," had no children.

❖

The greyhound is the fastest dog in the world, clocked at 41.7 miles per hour.

❖

According to an intelligence test of 79 dog breeds, the smartest is the Border Collie.

❖

In humans, the right lung weighs more than the left.

❖

The most common noncontagious disease is tooth decay.

Quick Quiz

In what two sports can a "perfect" game occur?

Baseball and bowling

NFL coaching legend Vince Lombardi coined the phrase "game plan."

❖

In 2005, Eric James Torpy was sentenced to 30 years in prison for robbery. A Larry Bird fan, Torpy asked that his term be 33 years to match his hero's jersey number. His wish was granted.

❖

T.S. Eliot's favorite gift to critics was exploding cigars.

❖

Listen up! About that ear that van Gogh cut off- it was his left one.

❖

Benjamin Franklin owned the first bathtub in the colonies. Good thing he didn't try the lightning experiment there.

❖

Confucius was not always a famous philosopher. At age 17 he was a corn inspector at the markets.

❖

Dolly Parton once lost a Dolly Parton look-alike contest.

Thoughts of the Throne

The Sunday Independent, a Wilkes-Barre, PA newspaper, once reported a story about a woman who returned home after a hospital stay "and found the first floor rear door to her home forced open. In a search of the home, the only article found missing was a four-pack of Charmin toilet tissue."

In skywriting, the average letter is nearly two miles high.

❖

The lobster automatically acquires a new form-fitting shell every year.

❖

The most popular seafood in America is shrimp. Tuna and salmon are tied for second.

❖

Stefani Germanotta is the real name of Lady Gaga.

❖

Jay-Z was born Shawn Corey Carter.

❖

Drake is the stage (and middle) name of Aubrey Graham.

❖

Amy Adams was once a Hooters girl.

❖

Lefthanders aren't allowed to play polo.

❖

Most people put on their left sock first.

Quick Quiz

In the 1800s, Dr. Miles' Compound Extract of Tomato was sold as a medicine. What do we know it as today?

Ketchup

There's a basketball court above the Supreme Court. They call it the Highest Court in the Land.

❖

Starburst fruit chews were originally known as Opal Fruits.

❖

The French call cotton candy "Papa's bread."

❖

Sylvester Graham, a vegetarian who lectured on healthy diets, created graham crackers.

❖

Washington, D.C., residents were not allowed to vote in presidential elections until the 23rd Amendment was ratified in 1961.

❖

Seoul, the South Korean capital, simply means "the capital" in the language of the land.

❖

Those symbols that cartoonists draw to replace epithets are called dingbats.

❖

Snickers is America's most popular candy bar.

Thoughts of the Throne

The first Charmin toilet paper commercial was filmed, appropriately, in Flushing, New York.

More than 90% of flowers have an unpleasant odor or no odor at all. Does that make scents?

❖

The April 1, 1985 issue of *Sports Illustrated* contained a cover article about Mets pitching prospect Sidd Finch, who threw a 168-mph fastball. It was an April Fool's joke.

❖

Danny Devito used to work as a hairdresser- for corpses.

❖

Scientists think that unborn babies can dream.

❖

The chance of a mother having quintuplets is 1 in 40,960,000.

❖

A male seal will go for three months at a stretch without food, drink or sleep.

❖

The average American laughs 15 times a day.

❖

Your nose and ears never stop growing.

Quick Quiz

Donald Duck's uncle, a bazillionaire, swims in his money bin in Duckburg. Name him.

Uncle Scrooge

In Ireland, a candle is placed in the window on Christmas Eve as a welcome light to all who might be seeking shelter.

❖

If you get stuck in an elevator during the holiday season, you have more chance of hearing *The Christmas Song* than any other sound of the season.

❖

A child's belief in Santa Claus peaks at age four.

❖

The Metropolitan Opera House in New York City is the largest opera house in the world.

❖

David Mullaney of Fairfield, Connecticut, invented the Wiffle Ball in 1953.

❖

If a female dog mates with more than one dog during her period of conception, it is possible for different puppies in her litter to have different fathers.

❖

One of Louis Pasteur's professors ranked him as barely mediocre in chemistry.

Thoughts of the Throne

When former President Lyndon B. Johnson was in the service during World War II, he was supposed to fly in the observation seat of the B-26 bomber Wabash Cannonball. It was shot down in New Guinea with no survivors. LBJ was replaced when he had to go to the bathroom before take-off.

New Orleans was awarded the Saints NFL franchise on November 1, 1966. Coincidentally, November 1 is known as "All Saints Day."

❖

When a black cat crosses your path in Japan, it means good luck.

❖

In Martin Van Buren's autobiography, the former president does not mention his wife.

❖

Ducks and geese can fly at a speed of 70 miles per hour in level flight. In uneven flight patterns, ducks tend to quack up.

❖

The longest flight of a cork from an unshaken champagne bottle is 177 feet, 9 inches.

❖

A jet plane has a point right behind the engine's exhaust where no sound at all is registered.

❖

During World War II, American G.I.s reported that Japanese soldiers would shout at them, "To hell with Babe Ruth!"

Quick Quiz

What's the only number that has the same amount of letters as its name?

Four

Facebook head honcho Mark Zuckerberg suffers from red-green color blindness. The color he can see best is blue, hence the predominant color of the website.

❖

The only day of the year the Washington Monument is closed is Christmas.

❖

In August 1911, Vincenzo Peruggia, an employee of the Louvre Museum, stole the Mona Lisa. He kept the painting for two years but was arrested when he tried to sell it.

❖

Rudyard Kipling paid off the nurse who cared for his child with the manuscript and rights to *The Jungle Book*.

❖

A whale has nostrils on top of its head.

❖

Three-fourths of all pencils sold in the U.S. are yellow-painted.

❖

The standard size of a credit card is 3 3/8" by 2 1/8."

Thoughts of the Throne

Donna Summer wrote *She Works Hard for the Money* about a bathroom attendant she found sleeping in a West Hollywood, California restaurant. The woman explained that she was totally spent from working two jobs.

Lamar Hunt coined the term "Super Bowl" for the NFL's championship game.

❖

Chinese checkers was invented in England in the 1800s and was originally called Halma.

❖

According to *The Guinness Book of World Records,* the most stolen book from a public library is-
The Guinness Book of World Records.

❖

The average American adult logs about 6.8 hours of shut-eye per night, or 2,482 hours a year. Wonder how much that is in winks? A wink takes 1/10 of a second. You do the math.

❖

Before "Hello" became the standard telephone greeting, folks said "Ahoy." Thomas Edison suggested the change.

❖

A standard U.S. passport has 24 pages.

❖

All llamas have bad breath- probably from yakking too much!

Quick Quiz

What TV family lives at 742 Evergreen Terrace?

The Simpsons

John Harrison holds a unique place in American history. He was both the father and son of a U.S. president- son of William Henry Harrison, elected president in 1840, and father of Benjamin Harrison, who became President of the U.S. in 1888.

❖

President Theodore Roosevelt's mother and wife both died, from unrelated causes, on the exact same day, February 14, 1884- Valentine's Day.

❖

Presidents Thomas Jefferson and John Adams both died on the exact same day in 1826- on the Fourth of July.

❖

President Grover Cleveland, when he was Sheriff of Erie County, New York, twice served as a hangman.

❖

Edgar Allan Poe was expelled from West Point in 1831 when he appeared at a parade in his birthday suit.

❖

When George Washington made the Marquis de Lafayette a major general in the Continental Army, the Frenchman was just 19 years old.

Thoughts of the Throne

Back in his heyday, former heavyweight boxing champ Mike Tyson spent 2.2 million dollars on a 24-karat gold bathtub.

Confederate General Stonewall Jackson's first name was Thomas.

❖

During the Civil War undertakers were called doctors.

❖

In 1969, *Midnight Cowboy* became the first and only X-rated film to win the Academy Award for Best Picture. (Its rating has since been changed to R.)

❖

Grover Cleveland had an artificial jaw made out of rubber. All politicians have been known to stretch a point but this was ridiculous.

❖

James Eggink was one of the Montreal Alouettes top choices in the 1996 Canadian Football League Draft. The problem? He died in December 1995.

❖

According to Gallup, 63% of dogs get Christmas presents from their owners, 58% of cats.

❖

In his lifetime, Thomas Edison patented 1,093 inventions.

Quick Quiz

Name the musician who was born Richard Starkey and gained worldwide fame as part of a rock band.

Ringo Starr

Henry F. Phillips invented the Phillips screw in 1936.

❖

Martha Washington was the first woman to appear on American paper currency.

❖

Salmon P. Chase is on the $10,000 bill.

❖

George Washington earned $25,000 a year as President of the U.S.

❖

The $1 bill is the most widely circulated paper currency in the U.S. Second is the $20 bill.

❖

Alexander Graham Bell never talked to his wife or mother on the telephone. They were both deaf.

❖

The original name for the portrait *Whistler's Mother* was *Arrangement in Grey and Black.*

❖

The White House was originally gray. It was burned during the War of 1812 and later rebuilt and painted white to cover the smoke stains.

Thoughts of the Throne

27,000 trees are wiped out every day to produce toilet paper.

Thomas Jefferson was the first man to be defeated in a presidential election.

❖

A leap year occurs every four years, in years evenly divisible by four, but a century year (which ends in two zeros like 1900, 2000, etc.) must also be evenly divided by 400. Got that?

❖

Bugs Bunny weighs 6 7/8 pounds.

❖

Nathan Ames invented the escalator in 1859.

❖

English muffins were first made in America, Venetian blinds were invented by the Chinese and the Belgians were the first to make French fries.

❖

The only two words in the English language that have all the vowels in their proper order are abstemiously and facetiously.

❖

If you have lost your marbles, head for the National Marbles Tournament, held annually in Wildwood, New Jersey.

Quick Quiz

What "Wall," built in 1982, was designed by 21-year-old Maya Lin?

The Vietnam Veterans Memorial, in Washington, D.C.

The only mammal that can fly is the bat.

❖

A duck has three eyelids.

❖

The "WD" in WD-40 stands for Water Displacement.

❖

The "B.F." in B.F. Goodrich is Benjamin Franklin.

❖

In 1911, hometown boy Ray Harroun won the first Indianapolis 500 with a blistering average speed of 74.6 miles per hour.

❖

The most common last name initial in the United States is "S."

❖

Alaska is almost three times the size of Texas.

❖

If you lift a kangaroo's tail off the ground it can't hop.

❖

There are 66 acceptable two-letter words in Scrabble.

Thoughts of the Throne

What do Elvis, Orville Redenbacher, Jim Morrison and Lenny Bruce have in common? They all went into the bathroom and never came out.

The first couple to be shown in bed together on primetime TV was Fred and Wilma Flintstone.

❖

While married, Sonny and Cher sometimes communicated by writing to each other in a diary left in their bathroom.

❖

Andrew Olsen invented the pop-up tissue box in 1921.

❖

William Shakespeare was born on April 23 and died 52 years later on April 23.

❖

The Indianapolis Motor Speedway, with a combined permanent seating and infield spectator capacity of over 400,000, is the largest sporting facility in the world.

❖

A mosquito has 47 teeth.

❖

Mosquitoes can drink twice their weight in blood.

❖

A mosquito's favorite aroma is aftershave.

Quick Quiz

What uniform number is retired throughout Major League Baseball?

42, in honor of Jackie Robinson

The Spanish national anthem has no words.

❖

Sir Walter Raleigh is buried with his favorite pipe and a tin of tobacco.

❖

Statistics show that Saturday is the most dangerous day to drive an automobile.

❖

The Russian word "kremlin" means "castle."

❖

Legendary songwriter Irving Berlin could not read music and could only play the black keys on a piano.

❖

Woodpeckers don't get headaches.

❖

Of the 3,000 islands that comprise the Bahamas chain in the Caribbean, only 20 are inhabited.

❖

A prairie dog isn't a dog. It's a rodent.

❖

The Red Sea is not red. It's bluish-green.

THOUGHTS OF THE THRONE

The first patent for rolled toilet paper was issued in 1883 to Seth Wheeler of Albany, New York. Before that, toilet paper was sold in flat sheets.

Hogs eat any and all kinds of snakes.

❖

A gnu has the feet of an antelope, the name and body of an ass, the head and humped shoulders of a buffalo and the beard of a goat.

❖

Opossums do not play dead. They are actually fainting.

❖

All polar bears are left-handed.

❖

Sir Winston Churchill was the first honorary citizen of the United States.

❖

Lyndon B. Johnson was known to conduct official business while in the bathroom at the White House.

❖

LBJ's favorite drink was Fresca. He had special taps installed in the White House to dispense the drink.

❖

The day after meeting Lady Bird, LBJ proposed. They were married two months later.

Quick Quiz

The Disney parks in California and Florida are, coincidentally, located in counties of the same fruitful name. What is it?

Orange County

The owl is a real bird-brain and not wise. Crows are thought to be the smartest birds.

❖

A hurricane, typhoon and cyclone are all the same thing.

❖

The French poodle originated in Germany.

❖

Dead people may not shiver, but they can get goose bumps.

❖

Former heavyweight boxing champion Leon Spinks was once mugged. The thugs made off with his money and jewelry- in addition to his two gold front teeth.

❖

A 1973 Macon, Georgia, minor league hockey team was named the Macon Whoopies after the song *Makin Whoopie.*

❖

Lee Trevino, Jerry Heard and Bobby Nichols were all struck by lightning during the same golf tournament in 1975.

Thoughts of the Throne

Science wanted to know, so taxpayers ponied up $100,000 to determine that three out of four Americans load their toilet paper with the flap in the front.

June 16, 1976, marked the first "rain-in" of a baseball game. The Houston Astros - Pittsburgh Pirates contest was called off because severe flooding made it impossible for fans to get to the Astrodome.

❖

The score of a forfeited NFL game is 2-0.

❖

J.K. Rowling's *Harry Potter* is the best-selling book series of all time, with more than 500 million books sold worldwide.

❖

Pigs look like they're tiptoeing because they walk on only two of four toes on each foot.

❖

When you breathe, the speed of your exhaled air is about 15 miles per hour.

❖

Seven letters in the English alphabet can double as Roman numerals- I, L, V, D, X, C and M.

❖

Thomas Edison was hard of hearing and often communicated with his wife in Morse code.

Quick Quiz

In 1987, who became the first woman inducted into the Rock and Roll Hall of Fame?

Aretha Franklin

It was (and maybe still is) illegal to wear roller skates in a Portland, Oregon, restroom.

❖

Arizona had a statute making it illegal to hunt camels in that state.

❖

In New York it is illegal to shoot at a rabbit from a moving trolley car.

❖

The *Pieta* was the only one of Michelangelo's sculptures that he signed.

❖

Leonardo da Vinci had trouble finishing anything. His interest would always wander to something else and he left a trail of partially completed works across Italy.

❖

James Whistler had to buy back his most famous painting, *Whistler's Mother*, from a pawn shop after his mother passed away.

❖

Each quill of the porcupine has about 1,000 tiny sharp barbs.

Thoughts of the Throne

The typical person visits the toilet six to eight times a day, or 2,500 times a year, spending three years there in an average lifetime.

A full-grown circus lion consumes about 30 pounds of horsemeat a day.

❖

A pig always sleeps on its right side.

❖

Former president George W. Bush met Laura at a backyard barbecue.

❖

Yes, there is a Hamburger Hall of Fame, and it's located in Seymour, Wisconsin.

❖

Former astronaut John Glenn and baseball great Ted Williams were co-pilots during Korean War bombing missions.

❖

Portland is the largest city in two different states.

❖

Manhole covers are made round because they can't fall through the manhole itself. Other shapes can.

❖

A stack of a trillion new one-dollar bills would reach 69,000 miles high.

Quick Quiz

What Australian airline is nicknamed the Flying Kangaroo?

Qantas

If you take a penny and double it, and then keep doubling it every day for 30 days, you will wind up with over five million dollars.

❖

The country of Paraguay doesn't use coins, just paper money.

❖

Mordecai Brown, one of the greatest pitchers in the history of baseball, had only three fingers on his pitching hand.

❖

The life span of a baseball in a Major League game is seven pitches.

❖

A female rabbit is called a doe; a male is a buck.

❖

Studies show that Americans favor pepperoni more than any other pizza topping.

❖

Elephants can get flat feet.

❖

Dr. Seuss coined the term "nerd."

Thoughts of the Throne

A whopping 75% of people use their mobile phone to text, talk and surf the web while they're in the bathroom.

Smithsonian Institution founder James Smith never set foot in the United States.

❖

The Union Army lost more men to disease than battle during the Civil War.

❖

Yankee Doodle was composed in England as an anti-American tune.

❖

According to the latest census, there are more than five million American natives in the U.S.

❖

Mary Phelps Jacobs patented the first brassiere in November of 1914.

❖

Back in Pilgrim days, a woman who reached the age of 30 and was unmarried was called a thornback.

❖

In 1901, Annie Taylor was the first woman to go over Niagara Falls in a barrel and survive.

❖

Chop Suey originated in California.

Quick Quiz

Who are the Duke and Duchess of Sussex? (Hint: Their son is Archie.)

Prince Harry and Meghan Markle

When Henry VIII became the King of England in 1509, he was only 17 years old.

❖

The Rolls Royce Corporation was founded in 1904 by two Englishmen, Rolls and Royce.

❖

The largest production car ever made was the 1927 Golden Bugatti. It measured 27 feet from bumper to bumper. Only six of these were ever made and a few are still around.

❖

The first person to be arrested for speeding was a New York City cab driver. On May 20, 1899, Jacob German was arrested for doing a breakneck 12 mph.

❖

Avon, the cosmetics giant, got its name because the founder was fond of Shakespeare, so the company was named after Stratford-on-Avon.

❖

Edgar Allan Poe often wrote his works with his cat seated on his shoulder.

❖

U.S. paper currency measures 6 1/8 by 2 9/16 inches.

Thoughts of the Throne

November 19 is World Toilet Day. Considering the time of year, some call it "Tanksgiving."

Greer Garson delivered the longest acceptance speech ever in the history of the Academy Awards when she won the Oscar for Best Actress in *Mrs. Miniver*. Her speech lasted 30 minutes.

❖

The first female cabinet member was Frances Perkins, appointed by FDR in 1933 as Secretary of Labor.

❖

Dogs are more likely to have a nervous breakdown than any other non-human animal.

❖

A group of swans is called a bevy.

❖

Gerald Ford was the only American president to have been a male model. He modeled winter sports clothes for *Look* magazine in 1939.

❖

The oldest bridegroom in history was Ralph Cambridge, who was 105 when he tied the knot with his 70-year-old bride, Adriana Kapp.

❖

Great Danes come from Germany, not Denmark.

Quick Quiz

In a deck of playing cards, how many eyes are on all four Jacks?

12

Turn of the 20th century multimillionaire Russell Sage amassed much of his money by never buying underwear. You could say he saved all his long john silver!

❖

The word "karate" means "empty hand."

❖

In a boxing match in 1923, Canadian flyweight champion Gene LaRue and challenger Kid Pancho simultaneously KO'd each other with haymaker lefts. The referee counted both fighters out.

❖

Sleepwalking is hereditary- and 2.5% of Americans do it regularly.

❖

Lady Randolph Churchill, Winston's mother, invented the Manhattan cocktail in 1874.

❖

In the 19th century, nine pins were used in bowling.

❖

U.S. presidents U.S. Grant, William Howard Taft, Herbert Hoover and Dwight D. Eisenhower never held any other elective office.

Thoughts of the Throne

In the 1930s, the Addis Brush Company created the first artificial brush trees for Christmas using the same machinery which made their toilet brushes.

Alligator shirts have crocodiles on them.

❖

If you think you eat like a bird, think again. Birds eat from one quarter to one half their bodyweight every day.

❖

Henry Wadsworth Longfellow is the only American whose bust is in Westminster Abbey.

❖

It doesn't matter what the birth certificate says in England; all royal birthdays are celebrated in June.

❖

Ernest Hemingway rewrote the last page of *A Farewell to Arms* 39 times.

❖

Architect Frank Lloyd Wright coined the word "carport."

❖

The largest fruit crop on Earth is grapes.

❖

Half the world's lemons grow in the United States, mostly in California.

Quick Quiz

Here's one that's elementary. What is Sherlock Holmes' assistant's first name?

John, my dear Watson

An avocado has 370 calories, the greatest number of any fruit.

❖

Pineapples are not native to Hawaii. They were first planted there in 1790.

❖

An excerpt from the diary of King George III of England stated, "Nothing of importance happened today." It was dated 7/4/1776.

❖

Calvin Coolidge was the only president to have been sworn in by his own father.

❖

Coolidge loved to fish but always wore gloves and made sure the Secret Service men handled the worms.

❖

When Oreo cookies were first made, they were mound-shaped. The name comes from the Greek word "oreo", which means "hill."

❖

Canada has more lakes than the rest of the world put together.

Thoughts of the Throne

Americans use 433 million miles of toilet paper a year. That's enough to stretch to the sun and back.

The average person's bones weigh 40 pounds.

❖

An adult's hair can stretch 25% of its length without breaking.

❖

According to *Harper's Index*, 80% of Americans believe in miracles.

❖

The odds of flipping a coin heads up ten times in a row are 1,023 to 1.

❖

Tug-of-war began as a sport in Ancient China.

❖

There has been only one Triple Crown winner that sired another Triple Crown winner. Gallant Fox was the father, Omaha the offspring.

❖

On June 19, 1989, "Bud" was the first tropical storm to be named after a male.

❖

The average winter temperature in Iceland is warmer than in Chicago.

Quick Quiz

What are the two shortest words which contain the first six letters of the alphabet?

Boldface and feedback

Ruth G. Wakefield invented the chocolate chip cookie in 1930.

❖

Caesar salad has nothing to do with the rulers of Rome. It was first made in a Tijuana bar in the twenties.

❖

Booker T. Washington was nicknamed "Booker" because of his love for books.

❖

Winnie-the-Pooh creator A. A. Milne's initials stand for Alan Alexander.

❖

John Greenwood was the dentist who made George Washington's false teeth.

❖

Dogs can understand about a 200-word human vocabulary while a cat comprehends only about 50 words.

❖

According to *Guinness*, the world's hardest tongue twister is this: "The sixth sick sheik's sixth sheep's sick."

Thoughts of the Throne

The toilet is flushed more times during Super Bowl halftime than at any time during the year.

The Alaskan flag was designed by a 13-year-old student who won an American Legion contest.

❖

Sports superstars have been honored by having their number retired. You, too, will have your day in glory. Your social security number will be permanently retired on the day you die.

❖

In 1950 the town of Hot Springs, New Mexico, renamed itself Truth or Consequences in honor of the former TV game show.

❖

Yes, Virginia, there is a Santa Claus. It's a town in Indiana. And, believe it or not, St. Nicholas Church is located there.

❖

The newspaper in Popeye's hometown of Sweethaven is called the *Sweethaven Daily Poop*.

❖

Howdy Doody's sister was named Heidi Doody.

❖

Dave Thomas, the founder of Wendy's, named the fast food restaurant after his daughter.

Quick Quiz

Name the most recent winner of horse racing's Triple Crown.

Justify, in 2018

Ida May Fuller of Vermont was the first person to receive a Social Security check. She got it in 1940 and lived to be over 100, eventually collecting more than $20,000.

❖

The last act at Woodstock was Jimi Hendrix.

❖

The national anthem of China is *March On, March On.*

❖

Goldie was Smokey Bear's mate. She bore him Smokey Bear II.

❖

The only dog that sweats is the Mexican hairless.

❖

The early bird may catch the worm but the poorwill catches a snooze. It is the only bird that hibernates.

❖

The average pro golfer whacks the ball at 194 mph.

❖

The delicious apple was originally called the Hawkeye.

Thoughts of the Throne

If you're ever motoring through the Lone Star State, remember the Alamo Heights Toilet Seat Art Museum, which displays 30 years of Barney Smith's greatest creations.

Eat a raw cashew and you may "cash-ew" in your chips. A cashew contains poisonous oil and needs to be roasted before it is safe for eating.

❖

The twin Popsicle was created during the Depression so that two children could share a single treat.

❖

According to the *New England Journal of Medicine*, if your left thumbnail is wider and squarer at the base than the right one, you're a southpaw (and vice-versa).

❖

Red schoolhouses were painted red for an elementary reason- it was the cheapest color.

❖

An ant's sense of smell is just as good as a dog's.

❖

The color red is not generally used in the packaging of ice cream because it reminds people of heat.

❖

The 1,500 pound leatherback turtle carries a shell that is as big as a king size bed, but a lot harder to find fitted sheets for.

Quick Quiz

What child's game originated in Sweden and was originally called "Anka Anka Gra Anka"?

Duck, Duck, Goose

An elephant smells through its mouth, not its trunk.

❖

A ticket to the best seat in the house for Super Bowl I went for $12. The price was considered exorbitant at the time and the game did not sell out at the Los Angeles Memorial Coliseum.

❖

1812 Overture composer Tchaikovsky suffered from nervous disorders, hallucinations and a morbid fear that his head would roll off his shoulders while conducting the orchestra.

❖

"Double hemisphere action" is the term used for the ability to write, simultaneously, something completely different with both your left and right hands.

❖

The three most popular cat names, in order, are Oliver, Bella and Simba.

❖

The longest recorded lifespan of a cat is 34 years.

❖

Red vs. white stripes on the U.S. flag? Reds win, 7-6.

Thoughts of the Throne

On April 23, 1978, a 25-pound green iceberg fell from the sky and landed in Ripley, Tennessee. The Federal Aviation Administration later reported that the ice mass was frozen waste that had fallen from a leaky airplane toilet.

Thomas Edison was 32 when he invented the light bulb.

❖

Al Capone carried a business card stating that he was "a secondhand furniture dealer."

❖

In 1938, Charles Zibbleman swam the Hudson River from Albany to New York City, traveling 147 miles and setting the record for handicapped swimmers. Zibbleman had no legs.

❖

The typical American eats 1,889 Tootsie Rolls in a lifetime.

❖

A watermelon is 92% water.

❖

Do you sleep in your birthday suit? 20% of men and 6% of women say they do.

❖

Walter Frederick Morrison invented the Frisbee, originally called the Pluto Platter, in 1948. When Morrison died in 2010, his family cremated him and turned his ashes into a Frisbee.

Quick Quiz

"The Statue of Liberty wear a size 879 sandal" is one of a ton of "Real Facts" found underneath the bottle caps of what soft drink?

Snapple

Americans love to "taste the rainbow", the slogan of Skittles, which is the number one non-chocolate selling candy in the U.S.

❖

You use 72 muscles to speak one word.

❖

Teddy Roosevelt owned a pet hyena named Bill.

❖

Cap'n Crunch's full name is Horatio Magellan Crunch.

❖

Barbie's full name is Barbie Millicent Roberts and her boyfriend Ken's last name is Carson.

❖

Whoopi Goldberg's real name is Caryn Johnson.

❖

Bill Cullen holds the record for hosting the most TV game shows- 20.

❖

The "Hollywood" sign in California was originally "Hollywoodland" but the last four letters fell down during World War II.

Thoughts of the Throne

Actor/comedian Chevy Chase, born Cornelius Crane Chase, is heir to the Crane Urinal fortune, so, as far as cash goes, you could say he is "flush."

Queen Elizabeth I suffered from smallpox and was completely bald by the age of 29.

❖

Arlington National Cemetery was once the site of Robert E. Lee's home.

❖

American Revolutionary War hero John Paul Jones became an admiral in the Russian Navy.

❖

Stubbs was the mayor of Talkeetna, Alaska, for 20 years, right up until his death in 2017. Stubbs was an orange cat.

❖

A woman can talk with less effort than a man because her vocal chords are shorter.

❖

A man's beard grows about an inch in eight weeks.

❖

Babies have over 60 more bones than adults.

❖

Blood takes about 23 seconds to make one round trip of your body.

Quick Quiz

Who was the only U.S. president that was a five-star general?

Dwight Eisenhower

60% of our body weight is water.

❖

There are 140 languages spoken around the world and each is spoken by more than one million people.

❖

The word "amen" is spoken in more tongues than any other word.

❖

The longest nonscientific word in the dictionary is floccinaucinihilipilification, a 29-letter term which means to decide if something has no value. (Maybe this word?)

❖

About one in six people is a habitual fingernail biter.

❖

Over half of all Americans wind up wearing some kind of corrective lenses.

❖

Movie trailers are so-called because they originally played after the film.

❖

A hippopotamus can outrun a man.

Thoughts of the Throne

When Sir Winston Churchill lost his seat in Parliament, someone saw fit to cable this message to him: "What good is a W.C. without a seat?"

It takes a skunk three weeks to crank out one ounce of foul odor.

❖

Silly statute: You can be fined for playing dominoes in Alabama on Sunday.

❖

Every citizen of Kentucky is required by law to take a bath once a year.

❖

Birds are even more warm-blooded than mammals. A body temperature of 108 degrees is not uncommon.

❖

Emperor penguins have square pupils.

❖

Black sheep have a keener sense of smell than white sheep.

❖

You can forget about the color red, as in cape, being a factor in bullfights. Bulls are colorblind.

❖

Canines with the best eyesight? Greyhounds rule.

Quick Quiz

What is Dorothy's last name in *The Wizard of Oz*?

Gale

People magazine selected Norma Jean Baker the Sexiest Woman of the 20th Century. You know her better as Marilyn Monroe.

❖

In the wintertime, squirrels lose about half of their nuts because they forget where they stored them.

❖

A crocodile can't stick its tongue out.

❖

Meteorologically speaking, partly cloudy and partly sunny means the same thing.

❖

CHOICE COD- Hold this upside-down in front of a mirror and you'll see that the first two words of this item read the same.

❖

Football historians claim the quarterback's exclamation of "hut" for the snap stems from Army drills where the drill sergeant would count off "Hut-2-3-4."

❖

Louis Pasteur was so obsessive about germs that he refused to shake hands with people.

Thoughts of the Throne

The National Aeronautics and Space Administration spent $23 million to build a prototype toilet for the space shuttle. The cost represented a 900 percent increase over the original estimate because the astronauts wanted a manual flush rather than an automatic one. Talk about true government waste!

The first live televised murder occurred in 1963, when Jack Ruby killed JFK's assassin, Lee Harvey Oswald.

❖

Maine is the only state surrounded on three sides by another country.

❖

At Four Corners you can walk in Utah, Colorado, Arizona and New Mexico within seconds.

❖

In the Philippine jungles, the yo-yo was first used as a weapon.

❖

The average American has a 10,000-word vocabulary.

❖

The average American woman owns seven pairs of jeans but only wears four on a regular basis.

❖

Beyonce has a horse fly named after her. Researchers named it "Scaptia beyonceae" because of the golden hairs on the fly's abdomen. They say it is the "all-time diva of flies."

Quick Quiz

What is the last name of TV psychologist Dr. Phil?

McGraw

Walt Disney considered Chesty, Tubby, Burpy, Deafy, Hickey, Wheezy and Awful before deciding to go with the Seven Dwarfs you know today.

❖

During the Korean War, baseball's Cincinnati Reds changed their name to the Redlegs for political reasons.

❖

George H.W. Bush, at 18, was the youngest Navy pilot of WWII.

❖

Just in case you weren't sure- Of the Wright brothers, it was Orville who made the first airplane flight, at 10:35 a.m. on December 17, 1903.

❖

King Camp Gillette created the safety razor with throwaway blades in 1895.

❖

The electric razor was invented by Jacob Schick in 1928.

❖

The average man spends about 3,500 hours shaving in his lifetime.

Thoughts of the Throne

In the circus or carnival world, a toilet is commonly referred to as a doniker.

A snake can hear with its tongue.

❖

Cold-blooded animals do not dream.

❖

Reindeer are superb swimmers.

❖

In 1993, Ireland's Eamonn Coghlan ran the mile in 3 minutes, 58.15 seconds, becoming the first man over 40 to run a mile in less than four minutes.

❖

A jogger's heel strikes the ground 1,500 times a mile.

❖

In the United States, a car is stolen every 30 seconds.

❖

The busiest phone number in New York City is 911, with 11,000,000 calls a year.

❖

A rat can go longer without water than a camel.

❖

Rats can't vomit.

QUICK QUIZ

The very first fast food restaurant opened in 1921 and the chain still exists today. Which franchise is first in the fast food order?

White Castle

Your skin weighs twice as much as your brain.

❖

The human tooth has approximately 50 miles of canals in it.

❖

Your heel is the body part least sensitive to pain.

❖

Christmas is celebrated with fireworks in Brazil.

❖

Last Chance Gulch, the 1860s mining camp, later changed its name to Helena and is now the capital of Montana.

❖

Florida's state song is *Old Folks at Home.*

❖

Nine-tenths of the ice in the world can be found in Antarctica.

❖

If you discount the "North" and "South" in the Americas, each of the world's continents begin and end with the same letter (e.g., EuropE, AmericA, AsiA).

Thoughts of the Throne

According to *Modern Bathrooms,* the most popular decoration on top of a toilet tank is scented seashells. Of course, we bathroom book publishers beg to differ.

The Gap clothing store chain opened in 1969 in San Francisco and was named by its owners, Donald and Doris Fisher, after the "generation gap."

❖

IBM was originally called the Computing-Tabulating-Recording Company.

❖

Nike was initially named Blue Ribbon Sports. The athletic shoemakers changed the name in 1968 to Nike after the Greek goddess of victory.

❖

The Washington Monument sinks an average of six inches a year.

❖

The presidential mansion in South Korea is known as the Blue House.

❖

The NBA's Utah Jazz team name stems from when they played in New Orleans.

❖

The Los Angeles Lakers name comes from Minnesota, the "Land of a Thousand Lakes," where they originally played.

Quick Quiz

Only four words end in "dous." How many can you name?

Hazardous, horrendous, stupendous and tremendous

A tuna can swim a hundred miles in one day.

❖

"Lampoon" is a French phrase meaning "Let's drink!"

❖

"Robot" comes from the Czech word for "slave."

❖

P.T. Barnum coined the phrase "Siamese twins."

❖

Carl Stotz invented Little League baseball.

❖

Joey Jay was the first Little Leaguer to play in the big leagues.

❖

The white shark has a perpetual appetite. No matter how much it eats, it is always hungry.

❖

A jellyfish that has been dead for months can still sting you if you walk on it in bare feet.

❖

Kool-Aid was originally called Fruit Smack.

Thoughts of the Throne

A Scott company employee saw a crumpled up roll of toilet paper and recognized its potential for another marketable product- a kind of disposable hand towel- thus the inspiration for paper towels.

The jawbone is the hardest bone in the body.

❖

Harvey Ball drew the first Smiley Face in 1963.

❖

John Landy was the second person to run a mile in under four minutes. Roger Bannister was first.

❖

The letter "t" is the second most commonly used letter in the English language. "E" is first.

❖

President Roosevelt nicknamed his political advisors the Tennis Cabinet.

❖

The President and Vice President of the United States are not allowed to travel together.

❖

Four out of five people who try out a new pen will write their own name.

❖

Americans buy around 2.7 billion boxes of cereal each year, enough to stretch all the way to the moon and back.

Quick Quiz

Which two NFL teams have won the most Super Bowls, with six apiece?

New England Patriots and Pittsburgh Steelers

Early watches had only one hand that indicated the hour.

❖

There are no clocks in gambling casinos.

❖

Bono's real name is Paul Hewson.

❖

Josephine Esther Mentzer underwent a cosmetic name change to Estee Lauder.

❖

It takes about a yard of sugar cane to make one sugar cube.

❖

It took an 1893 Supreme Court ruling to declare the tomato a vegetable rather than a fruit.

❖

In 1915, the average annual American family income was $687.

❖

The average magazine lies around the house for 29 weeks before someone gets around to throwing it out.

Thoughts of the Throne

A hibernating bear can go as long as six months without, well, going.

There are 575 words in the epic poem *Casey at the Bat.*

❖

Two out of three people can name the three Rice Krispies characters.

❖

U.S. coffee consumers drink an average of 3.2 cups per day.

❖

Rice is eaten by one half of all the people in the world every day.

❖

Deviled eggs are so-called because when they were first made, they were covered with such hot pepper that it supposedly reminded one of the fires of Hell.

❖

The higher a plane flies, the less fuel it uses as the atmosphere is thinner and the vehicle meets less resistance.

❖

The wingspan of a Boeing 747 is greater than the entire flying distance of the Wright Brothers famous first foray into the wild blue yonder.

Quick Quiz

In Spanish, it's an affectionate term for a little girl. Worldwide, it's arguably the most famous banana trademark. What is it?

Chiquita

A penguin is the only bird that can swim but not fly.

❖

The largest flying bird is the albatross.

❖

The Vice President of the U.S. lives at Number One Observatory Circle, on the grounds of the United States Naval Observatory in Washington, D.C.

❖

In *I Love Lucy*, the Ricardos lived at 623 East 68th Street in Manhattan.

❖

1 Cherry Street in New York City was home to George Washington as it was the first U.S. presidential address.

❖

14% of Americans move each year.

❖

If you're suffering from sphenopalatine ganglioneuralgia, in just plain English, you have an ice cream headache.

❖

Big Bird has a teddy bear named Radar.

Thoughts of the Throne

The average male who shaves regularly will use up five months of his life doing so, removing 28 feet of hair.

The bite of a cobra is deadly enough to kill even an elephant if it's bitten on the trunk tip or the base of the toenail.

❖

Tombstones were originally placed on plots over the dead so that the deceased could not come out and harm the living.

❖

Rocker Rod Stewart was once a gravedigger.

❖

Alfred Blozis set the world record for the hand grenade toss back in 1944 when he lobbed the old pineapple 284.5 feet.

❖

The White House is the most visited home in the United States. Second is Graceland, the former home of Elvis Presley, in Memphis, Tennessee.

❖

60% of Americans own dogs, 47% have cats in their household, and 8% have birds.

❖

When the mood of an octopus changes, so does its color.

Quick Quiz

What sport was originally called mintonette and was invented by William Morgan in Holyoke, MA, in 1895?

Volleyball

A cow spends approximately 18 out of every 24 hours chewing on something.

❖

The leader of a wolf pack is always female.

❖

J.C. Penney's middle name was Cash.

❖

Sam Walton's first job was at J.C. Penney.

❖

The phrase "stone broke" comes from the Middle Age custom of breaking stone benches of craftsmen who were unable to pay their debts.

❖

There are more words in the English language than any other language in the world.

❖

Johann Sebastian Bach fathered 20 children.

❖

There are 20 possible moves in chess.

❖

Sponge Bob's first name is Robert.

Thoughts of the Throne

A 2017 survey of 4,000 people found that 63% of the people in America like doing what you may be doing right now- reading in the bathroom.

Salvador Dali avoided paying restaurant tabs by using checks. He would draw on the back of them as the waiter watched, knowing full well that they'd never cash the art.

❖

Pink has a bar code tattooed on the back of her neck.

❖

The first newspaper crossword puzzle, by Arthur Wynne, appeared in the *New York World* on December 21, 1913.

❖

The first supermarket was established in 1916 when Clarence Saunders set up shop with the Piggley Wiggley self-service food mart in Memphis, Tennessee.

❖

Gene Conley is the only athlete to play on world championship teams in both Major League Baseball and the NBA.

❖

Transsexual Renee Richards (nee Richard Raskind) is the only tennis player to compete in both the men's and women's singles at the U.S. Open.

Quick Quiz

Name the three states spelled with only four letters.

Iowa, Ohio and Utah

Lewis Carroll wrote *Alice's Adventures in Wonderland* standing up.

❖

Henry David Thoreau's last words, uttered on May 6, 1862, were "Moose, Indian." Their meaning is unknown.

❖

Ventriloquist Edgar Bergen (and his dummy, Charlie McCarthy) received the only wooden Oscar.

❖

If the coils of the French horn were straightened out, the instrument would be 22 feet long.

❖

A clothes designer in New Jersey once designed a jacket with 89 zippers.

❖

George Washington gave New York the nickname of the "Empire State."

❖

Fairy tale writer Hans Christian Anderson was dyslexic. Others afflicted by dyslexia include Thomas Edison, Woodrow Wilson, Tom Cruise and Henry Winkler.

Thoughts of the Throne

In observance of National Toilet Paper Day, annually on August 26, the folks at Charmin manufactured the world's largest toilet paper roll ever. Eight feet high and nine feet wide, the monstrous roll was made out of 1,000,000 square feet of toilet paper- the equivalent of 95,000 regular toilet rolls!

Three out of four Americans like to doodle.

❖

Aesop was believed to have been a dwarf.

❖

An ostrich can cover 25 feet in a single stride.

❖

Most hummingbirds weigh less than a penny.

❖

To bankers, ZIP is an acronym for Zero Interest Payment.

❖

To psychologists, ZIP is short for Zero Intelligence Potential.

❖

To postal workers, ZIP stands for Zoning Improvement Plan.

❖

A butterfly flaps its wings about 300 times a minute.

❖

In Tiddlywinks, the art of flipping the winks into a cup is called "Potting."

Quick Quiz

"The cheese stands alone" is the last line of what nursery rhyme?

The Farmer in the Dell

Retlaw Yensid was the writer of the 1966 Disney movie *Lt. Robin Crusoe, U.S.N.* Retlaw Yensid is Walter Disney backwards.

❖

"Chop suey" means "odd and ends."

❖

In colonial America, lobster wasn't exactly a delicacy. It was so inexpensive and readily available that it was often served to prisoners.

❖

A hockey rink is 200 feet long.

❖

"Jack" is the most common name in nursery rhymes.

❖

The only one of the seven dwarfs who is beardless is Dopey.

❖

Employees at Disney World were not allowed to wear mustaches up until 2000.

❖

Children under age 4 and adults over 50 rarely blush.

Thoughts of the Throne

Studies show that the stall closest to the door in a public restroom is usually the cleanest and least-used.

Jack Nicholson single-handedly rescued five drowning people from the New Jersey surf back in the 1950s.

❖

The first drive-in theater opened in 1932 in Camden, New Jersey.

❖

Cacophobia is a fear of ugliness.

❖

Bibliophobia is a fear of books.

❖

The longest-named phobia we came across was macroxenoglossophobia- a fear of long words!

❖

"Mind Your Business" was the motto printed on one of the first U.S. coins.

❖

Adolf Hitler was a vegetarian.

❖

Before getting into politics, Fidel Castro was a movie extra in Hollywood and made a film with Esther Williams.

Quick Quiz

There are 88 keys on a piano. How many are white and how many are black?

52 white, 36 black

Robert Todd Lincoln was present at three presidential assassinations- his father's, President Garfield's and President McKinley's.

❖

Kleenex tissues were first used as a filter in gas masks during World War I.

❖

At the outbreak of WWI, the American Air Force consisted of only 50 men. Of course, that wasn't so bad considering they only had one plane!

❖

Hot Foot Teddy was Smokey Bear's original name.

❖

In 1952, Queen Elizabeth was named *Time* magazine's "Man of the Year."

❖

Former President John Tyler joined the Confederacy and thus became the only Chief Executive ever to become a sworn enemy of the United States.

❖

Frank Lloyd Wright, the famous architect, also had a hand in designing one of the biggest movie stars of the fifties. Ann Baxter is his granddaughter.

THOUGHTS OF THE THRONE

The most germs on your toilet are on the handle. Still in all, cell phones have 18 times more bacteria than toilet handles.

Some laws, which were (and may still be) on the books - In Memphis, Tennessee, it's against the law for frogs to croak after 11 P.M.

❖

It's illegal to ride a bike into a swimming pool in Baldwin Park, California.

❖

You must leave your shoes on if your feet smell while in the theater in Winnetlea, Illinois.

❖

Most of the germs that get into your body enter through your mouth.

❖

The blood of a spider is transparent.

❖

A man with more than one wife is a polygamist. A woman with more than one husband is a polyandrist.

❖

Washington, D.C. has the highest ration of lawyers per resident- one for every 12 people.

❖

Pumpkins are actually a fruit.

Quick Quiz

What is the plural of the word "moose"?

Moose

DaVinci's masterpiece, *Mona Lisa*, took ten years to complete.

❖

The best-selling art poster in America is van Gogh's *Starry Night*.

❖

van Gogh signed his paintings with his first name, Vincent.

❖

Rin Tin Tin and Lassie have prints on the Hollywood Walk of Fame.

❖

President John Quincy Adams had a pet alligator in the White House.

❖

The only animal to be awarded both the Purple Heart and Silver Star during World War II was Chips, a K-9 dog.

❖

The only street in the world to claim two Nobel Peace Prize winners is in Soweto in South Africa. Nelson Mandela and Archbishop Desmond Tutu both have abodes in Vilakazi Street, Orlando West.

Thoughts of the Throne

Television host and comic Howie Mandel was once the butt of a practical joke when his California house was TP'd with more than 4,000 rolls of toilet paper. The perpetrators were TV prankster Roman Atwood and Mandel's own son.

"You dirty rat" is a line attributed to James Cagney, but never used by him in any movie.

❖

Roy Rogers is the only person ever elected to the Country Music Hall of Fame twice.

❖

Rocky Lane, a cowboy film actor, was the voice of that talking horse, Mr. Ed.

❖

The strawberry is a member of the rose family and is the only fruit to have its seeds on the outside.

❖

Albert Einstein never wore socks.

❖

Einstein was offered the presidency of Israel in 1952 but turned it down.

❖

Edward Craven Walker invented the Lava Lamp in 1963.

❖

If you like to engage in many sesquipedalianisms, you like to use big words.

Quick Quiz

Who's the current host of the longest-running game show in TV history, *The Price is Right*?

Drew Carey

Three different numbers give the same result when added together as when multiplied. You know what they are, don't you? It's as easy as 1, 2, 3.

❖

Elvis was once appointed Special Agent of the Bureau of Narcotics and Dangerous Drugs.

❖

It wasn't until the Civil War that specific left and right shoes were made.

❖

National Park Services policy prohibits acts of violence or death scenes to be filmed in front of Mount Rushmore.

❖

The inventors of Pepsi, Coke and Dr Pepper were all Civil War veterans.

❖

The Indian on the Indian head penny was not an Indian at all. The model was a relative of one of the mint's officials.

❖

The elephant is the only animal that can't jump and the only animal with four knees.

Thoughts of the Throne

The first toilet flush heard on television came from Archie Bunker's upstairs bathroom on *All in the Family*.

Charles Lindbergh was not the first person to cross the Atlantic in an airplane. Sixty-six people made the trip before he did. He was the first to fly alone.

❖

As many as 100 pearls have been found in a single oyster.

❖

The ice covering the Arctic Ocean is 7 to 10 feet thick.

❖

Jerry Seinfeld sold light bulbs by telephone.

❖

The Far Side's Gary Larson once ran over a dog on his way to a job interview with the Seattle Humane Society. He got the job and became an animal abuse investigator.

❖

James Madison was the first president to wear long pants; his predecessors all wore knickers.

❖

Pink lemonade was created in 1857 by Pete Conklin, who unwittingly used a bucket of water in which a circus performer had soaked his red tights.

QUICK QUIZ

What building is on the back of a five-dollar bill?

The Lincoln Memorial

The most common name for a town in the United States is Franklin.

❖

When asked to name a color, the most common answer is "red."

❖

The most common albino animal is the Siamese cat.

❖

Abraham Lincoln was a licensed bartender.

❖

About 400,000,000 M&Ms are sold each day. They may come in many different colors but as far as dentists go, that means a lot of green.

❖

Until the 1960s, men with long hair were not allowed in Disneyland. Yeah... but they let Donald Duck run around the place with no pants.

❖

A giraffe has the same number of bones in its neck as a human.

❖

Up to 8% of men are deficient in color vision.

Thoughts of the Throne

Each year there are more than 40,000 toilet-related injuries in the United States.

Bananas can get "sunburned." The resulting dark brown or black spots look like, but are not necessarily, a sign of over-ripeness.

❖

The biggest consumers of coffee in the world, per capita, are Finland, Norway and Iceland.

❖

In 2018, Steve Geddes of Boscawen, New Hampshire, grew the largest pumpkin ever recorded in U.S. history- weighing in at 2,528 pounds.

❖

The "Umbrella Girl" of the Morton Salt Company and her accompanying slogan - "When it rains, it pours," made their first appearance in 1911.

❖

About 20 to 30 volcanoes erupt each year, mostly under the sea.

❖

In 1967, the Monkees outsold both the Beatles and the Stones.

❖

In 1970, Diane Crump became the first female jockey in the Kentucky Derby.

Quick Quiz

What do arctophiles collect?

Teddy bears

On the very day Lincoln was assassinated, John Wilkes Booth stalked General Grant's wife, Julia. The Grants declined the invitation to go to Ford's Theater that evening and went instead to visit their children.

❖

Both of James Madison's vice presidents died while in office.

❖

The eggplant is actually a berry.

❖

In the 16th century, bread was portioned out by status. Laborers or servants got the burnt bottom of the loaf, the family got the middle, and guests enjoyed the top, or as we refer to them today, the "upper crust."

❖

Researchers at Purdue University reported that their licking machine, modeled after a human tongue, required an average of 364 licks to get to the center of a Tootsie Pop.

❖

The most popular toothbrush color in America is blue.

Thoughts of the Throne

London's Wembley Stadium has more toilets than any other venue in the world- 2,618.

If Swanson hadn't been stuck with a huge load of turkey on Thanksgiving, 1953, it may never have developed the first TV dinner in 1954.

❖

On average, 90% of Dutch teenagers can speak English fluently. Only 80% of American teenagers can say the same.

❖

When he graduated from West Point, Ulysses S. Grant had no intention of making the military his career and looked forward instead to the rather dull life of a professor of mathematics.

❖

In 1978, Janet Parker, a medical photographer, became the last person known to die of smallpox.

❖

Boxing great Sugar Ray Robinson was originally tagged with the moniker Walker Smith Jr.

❖

Tom Cruise was born Thomas Mapother IV.

❖

Beaver, Oklahoma, is known as the Cow Chip Throwing Capital of the World.

Quick Quiz

What comedian hosted *Saturday Night Live* when it made its debut November 11, 1975, on NBC?

George Carlin

Dr Pepper was named after a real doctor in Virginia who gave the drink's inventor, Wade Morrison, his first job. By the way, there's no period after the "Dr" in "Dr Pepper."

❖

The daily heat output of the human body is enough to boil eight gallons of freezing water.

❖

There's a law in Rochester, Michigan, that anyone bathing in public must have their bathing suit inspected by a police officer. Apparently, the town doesn't give people enough credit to tell right from thong.

❖

Among the Beatles, Paul McCartney and Ringo Starr were left-handed.

❖

Pope John Paul II was once named an "Honorary Harlem Globetrotter." With that hat, he'd have made a great shot blocker.

❖

The only battle fought on American soil since the Civil War was the One Thousand Mile War in 1943, when Japan invaded the Aleutian Islands.

Thoughts of the Throne

Televisions are more popular than toilets in Afghanistan. 90% of homes are equipped with TVs, only 7% with toilets.

The presidential residence has only been known as the "White House" since 1901, when it was officially named so by Teddy Roosevelt.

❖

There are over 3,000 species of mosquitoes. That's a lot of bloodsuckers even if you don't count politicians.

❖

Scuba divers cannot pass gas below 33 feet.

❖

Beachcombers beware! It's a federal rap to disturb a dead whale.

❖

John Glenn was the oldest American to go into space- twice.

❖

Jamie Foxx's birth name was Eric Bishop.

❖

Israeli postage stamp glue is certified kosher.

❖

Riding a merry-go-round on Sunday in Idaho is illegal.

Quick Quiz

What's the only state capital that is made up of three words?

Salt Lake City (Utah)

On March 29, 1848, for the first time in history, Niagara Falls stopped flowing. An ice jam above the rim of the falls caused the water to stop.

❖

If the doctor tells you that you are suffering from graphospasms and scrivener's palsy, don't worry. That's just his $200 way of informing you that you have writer's cramp.

❖

The White House has survived two major fires: one during the War of 1812 and the other in 1929, during Herbert Hoover's presidency.

❖

Elvis Presley made his Las Vegas debut at the Frontier Hotel on April 22nd, 1956. He didn't go over well with the middle-aged crowd and was fired a week later.

❖

In the first four months of 2007, golfer Jacqueline Gagne sank 10 holes-in-one. The odds of this happening are estimated to be 1 out of 670,000,000,000,000,000,000.

❖

A 2x4 is really 1.5 by 3.5.

Thoughts of the Throne

An all-important statistical survey found that 88% of Americans say they'd replace an empty roll of toilet tissue rather than leave the chore to the next person.

43% of all beer sold is consumed by just 10% of beer drinkers.

❖

President Franklin Roosevelt once forgot his dog Fala and left him behind on a remote Alaskan island. He taught the Navy to play "fetch" as he dispatched a destroyer to pick him up.

❖

You knew it was true. You could feel it. Every day is longer than the day before it- by about 55 billionths of a second.

❖

The names of Popeye's four nephews are Pipeye, Peepeye, Pupeye and Poopeye.

❖

Facebook engineers originally wanted to call the "Like" button the "Awesome" button.

❖

University of Oregon student Carolyn Davidson designed the Nike logo in 1964. She was paid $35 for the design.

❖

Play-Doh was originally used as wallpaper cleaner.

Quick Quiz

Who are Bruce Wayne and Dick Grayson?

Batman and Robin, respectively

The first patent for chewing gum was issued to William F. Semple in 1869.

❖

Every person has a tongue print as individual as fingerprints, so if you're going safecracking, wear gloves and resist the urge to lick the dial.

❖

More than 90% of the trade between nations is carried by ship.

❖

People were much shorter in Revolutionary times. Doorways from that period barely offered five feet of clearance.

❖

The hibernating artic ground squirrel has antifreeze in its blood and is thus the only mammal able to survive freezing temperatures.

❖

Once a fixture on TV, the last cigarette commercial was shown on Johnny Carson's *Tonight Show* on January 1st, 1971.

❖

Nepal is the only nation without a rectangular flag.

Thoughts of the Throne

Axillary hyperhidrosis is usually treated in the bathroom. That's what your antiperspirant is for.

A good deal of Florida's air pollution comes from dust blowing in from Africa.

❖

The average cat consumes about 127,750 calories a year, nearly 28 times its own weight.

❖

Johnson & Johnson began marketing the band-aid bandage in 1921.

❖

If you stretched out a single human DNA molecule, it would be 5 feet, 5 inches long.

❖

The estimated age of the world's oldest crow is 118 years.

❖

There are more than 43,252,003,274,489,856,000 possible positions for a Rubik's Cube.

❖

William Herschel discovered the planet Uranus in 1781 and named it Georgium Sidium in honor of King George III of England. In 1850, it was renamed Uranus, thereby assuring snickers for generations to come.

Quick Quiz

The Antoinette Perry Awards for Excellence in Theatre are commonly referred to by what name?

The Tony Awards

Garnet Carter built the world's first miniature golf course on Lookout Mountain in Tennessee in 1927.

❖

For 67 consecutive years, Mary was America's most popular female baby name. Linda broke the streak in 1947. Emma, Olivia and Ava are the top three names for girls today.

❖

McDonald's once made bubble gum-flavored broccoli.

❖

Here's an important number to remember: there are seven loops in the squiggle atop a Hostess cupcake.

❖

A mouse can squeeze through a hole the size of a ballpoint pen.

❖

Happy Birthday was the first song performed in outer space, by the Apollo IX astronauts on March 8, 1969.

❖

A squirrel's tail can be used as a parachute, enabling it to fall up to 100 feet without injury.

Thoughts of the Throne

It wasn't only the shower scene in *Psycho* that was historic. The film was the first American movie ever to show a toilet flushed on screen.

First prize at the Wife Carrying World Championships in Finland is the wife's weight in beer.

❖

A labeorphilist is a beer bottle collector.

❖

The only First Lady born outside the U.S. besides Melania Trump was Louisa Adams, wife of John Q.

❖

James Garfield was the only U.S. president to have been an ordained minister.

❖

If you've ever dreamed of climbing Mt. Everest, better hurry- it's getting taller by about a half-an-inch to one inch every year.

❖

You probably always thought it was the Spirit of 76, but an act of Congress declared bourbon the official spirit of the USA.

❖

Peter Boyle, most famous for playing Frank Barone in the sitcom *Everybody Loves Raymond*, was best man at John Lennon's wedding.

Quick Quiz

This country singer was best known for *Achy Breaky Heart*, but may now be better-known as the father of a famous daughter. Name him.

Billy Ray Cyrus- His daughter, of course, is Miley Cyrus.

An irrational fear of wine is called oenophobia.

❖

The top-selling wine in the United States is Chardonnay.

❖

Cats have as many as 245 bones before they fuse together. Maybe that's why dogs chase them so much.

❖

58% of cat owners are women.

❖

Gorillas can't swim.

❖

Cotton Candy was invented by a dentist.

❖

PEZ is short for pfefferminz, the German word for "peppermint." PEZ dispensers with character heads have been pumping out the compact candies since 1952.

❖

Boomer icons Janis Joplin, Jimi Hendrix and Jim Morrison were all 27 when they died.

Thoughts of the Throne

A German toilet paper maker manufactured a brand of paper imprinted with a 26 lesson language course in English.

Cows don't have upper front teeth.

❖

India has a Bill of Rights for cows. That comes in handy in case anybody has a beef.

❖

Not just any corn can be popcorn. It requires a variety with extra moisture inside to generate the steam which causes the corn to pop.

❖

An elephant can drink 15,000 gallons of water in one year.

❖

Henry Ford, his pal Thomas Edison and Ford's cousin's husband, E.G. Kingsford, came up with the idea for charcoal briquettes in the 1920s. What did you come up with during your last barbeque?

❖

Actress Reese Witherspoon is a direct descendant of John Witherspoon, one of the 56 signers of the Declaration of Independence.

❖

A survey among florists revealed that men tend to buy red flowers more than any other color.

Quick Quiz

What's the name of the rooster on the Kellogg's Cornflakes box?

Cornelius, or Corny for short

Karaoke means "empty orchestra" in Japanese.

❖

Dogs and humans are the only animals with prostates. That probably explains why each species has a similar reaction to hearing the snap of a rubber glove.

❖

The microwave oven is used more for reheating coffee than for any other reason.

❖

The one millionth trademark from the U.S. Patent Office was granted to Sweet 'N Low.

❖

The average American eats more lettuce than any other vegetable, an average of 25.8 pounds per year.

❖

A typical four-year-old child asks over 400 questions a day.

❖

Bic pens were originally to be named after inventor Marcel Bich but marketers dropped the "h" when they realized how the name might be pronounced in America.

Thoughts of the Throne

A leading toilet paper manufacturer's survey found that 7% of Americans steal toilet paper from public bathrooms.

Tonsurphobia is a fear of haircuts.

❖

In 1985, a buyer paid well over $200,000 for a bottle of 1787 Chateau Lafitte claret engraved with the initials of Thomas Jefferson. About a year later, the cork dried out and turned it into the most expensive vinegar of all time.

❖

Cats can see about six times better than humans.

❖

The Russians showed up 12 days late to the 1908 Olympics in London because they were using the Julian calendar instead of the Gregorian calendar.

❖

If you live in Los Angeles and want to pop up to Reno for a bit of action on the gaming tables, you'll have to head west.

❖

Nearly half of all notes printed by the Bureau of Engraving and Printing are one-dollar bills.

❖

Seahorses are monogamous life mates. They travel in pairs, holding each other's tails.

Quick Quiz

How many rows of stars spangle a U.S. flag?

Nine

The first oranges were green.

❖

Despite credit on the labels, Elvis did not write nor co-write any of his songs.

❖

Penguins spend approximately 75% of their life in the water.

❖

Blood makes up about 7% of your body's weight.

❖

B.F. Goodrich coined the term "zipper." Up until then, they had been called "separable fasteners."

❖

If Charles Lindbergh's grandfather hadn't changed the family's last name, the famed flier would have been known as Charles Manson.

❖

Banana peels make excellent fertilizer for rose bushes.

❖

Multi-billionare Warren Buffet eats at McDonald's every single morning.

Thoughts of the Throne

Until December, 1978, a Connecticut regulation required all toilets to have horseshoe-shaped seats.

Despite its name, the black bear can actually be chocolate, white, blonde or cinnamon in color.

❖

Blue can whales eat up to a half-million calories in a mouthful.

❖

Whales not only communicate, they speak in dialects.

❖

Mickey Mouse's nephews are Morty and Ferdy.

❖

The original voice of Mickey Mouse was Walt Disney.

❖

In 1974, the *Journal of Applied Behavior Analysis* published a paper titled "The Unsuccessful Self-Treatment of a Case of 'Writer's Block.'" It contained no words.

❖

Before St. Paul, Minnesota, became the state capital, it was named "Pig's Eye."

❖

Honey never spoils.

Quick Quiz

What was Mario's original name before the *Super Mario Bros.* video game series?

Jumpman

In 16th century Denmark, cheese was often used as currency. Perhaps you had to go to a bank when you wanted a "Provo-loan."

❖

Over his or her lifetime, the average person walks 115,000 miles.

❖

A study done by the *Journal of the American Medical Association* found that 32% of studies are inaccurate.

❖

If you ever wondered why Charlie Brown's hair was always like that, his father was a barber.

❖

The average American spends six years of their life in the bathroom and only six months at stoplights. So, which do you think involves more stop and go?

❖

Cookie Monster's real name is Sid.

❖

Bob Griese of the Miami Dolphins was the first NFL quarterback to wear glasses in a game. His spectacles are on display in the sport's Hall of Fame.

Thoughts of the Throne

70% of Americans say they close the bathroom door even when no one else is home.

Gone with the Wind was Margaret Mitchell's only novel.

❖

The only country whose national flag is a single color is Libya. It's green.

❖

Calvin Coolidge was the only U.S. president born on a national holiday, July 4, 1872.

❖

There's only one U.S. state capital without a McDonald's, and that's Montpelier, Vermont.

❖

Some of the vanity license plates that have appeared on the Oscar Mayer Weinermobile include YUMMY, OURDOG, WEENR, and BIG BUN.

❖

There are as many Italians in Toronto, Canada, as in Venice, Italy.

❖

France originated kilts.

❖

When a gorilla is angry, it sticks its tongue out.

Quick Quiz

What four-letter media giant is located in Bristol, Connecticut?

ESPN

If you go on a wine tasting tour in Utah, it is against the law to swallow the wine.

❖

The state of Minnesota forbids crossing state lines with a duck on your head.

❖

The total weight of termites on Earth exceeds the total weight of humans. Nevertheless, you never see a termite worried about dieting.

❖

Ben & Jerry's has an online graveyard for their discontinued ice cream flavors. It shows a photo, lifespan, and epitaph for each one.

❖

Jerry Seinfeld reportedly declined an offer of $5 million per episode to continue *Seinfeld*.

❖

Nicki Minaj, whose real name is Onika Tanya Maraj, suffers from acrophobia, meaning she's afraid of heights.

❖

Jorge Mario Bergoglio was a nightclub bouncer who you know better today as Pope Francis.

Thoughts of the Throne

Alaska lays claim to being the state with the most outhouses in the U.S.

If bodies to the same scale were put on the presidential heads at Mt. Rushmore, they would each stand 465 feet tall.

❖

There were four U.S. presidents who lost the popular vote but won the electoral college vote-Rutherford Hayes, Benjamin Harrison, George W. Bush and Donald Trump.

❖

President James Madison never weighed over a hundred pounds.

❖

Martin Van Buren, who coined the term "okay," was the first president born an American citizen.

❖

Warren G. Harding lost the White House china in a poker game.

❖

There's a town in Missouri called Peculiar. Its motto is, "Where the odds are with you."

❖

The four least-used letters of the alphabet, in order of their infrequency, are Q, X, Z and J.

Quick Quiz

How many feet are there in a mile?

5,280

The "E." in Chuck E. Cheese stands for "Entertainment."

❖

The inventor of the "best before" dates, which was originally for milk, was Al Capone.

❖

There are 2,598,960 different poker hands possible in a deck of cards.

❖

Lady Gaga taught herself to play piano at age four.

❖

"Money can't buy life" were the last words of singer/songwriter Bob Marley, to his son Ziggy.

❖

San Francisco has the largest Chinese population outside the Orient.

❖

A humpback whale can travel up to 4,000 miles in a year.

❖

In 1927, a telephone call from New York to London cost $75 for the first three minutes.

Thoughts of the Throne

On an episode of *Married...with Children*, main character Al Bundy constructed his ideal bathroom, which included five rolls of toilet paper and no sink.

The Bathroom Library

The Bathroom Football Almanac

The Bathroom Joke Almanac

The Bathroom Sports Almanac

The Bathroom Trivia Almanac

The Bathroom Fascinating Facts Book

The Bathroom Game Book

The Bathroom Golf Book

The Bathroom Laugh Out Loud Book

For more information:

Email - info@Red-LetterPress.com
Website - www.Red-LetterPress.com